D1284355

Randy Benjamin

How To Publish Anything On
Amazon's Kindle

Also by Randy Benjamin (Nonfiction)

The Healthy Computer (DVD Only)
The Internet Guide Handbook
More of the Internet Guide

Randy Benjamin writing as Asher Dan (Fiction)

The Anomaly
Tapestries (Children's album and book)

How To Publish Anything
On Amazon's Kindle

An Intguide Publication / December 2008

Subsidiary Rights
Randy Benjamin
60 Thompson Drive
Vincennes, IN 47591

www.RandyBenjamin.com
ISBN 978-0-9679361-2-3

Printed in the United States of America

How To Publish Anything
On Amazon's Kindle

Before we get started, there is one thing I should say. I noticed that someone has complained in a review that this book didn't help him to publish a Power Point presentation. Well, DUH! I mean, it won't help you convert your text to French either. Power point presentations can't be converted to the Kindle format. Or any other e-book format that I'm aware of. So, if you're trying to do something that can't be done, then NO, this book isn't going to be of any use to you. But in about 99% of the other cases...it will be.

Actually, if you find that you can't get something to work and you think it should, email me at: www.randybenjamin.com and I'll see if I can answer your questions. That said, let's continue.

Virtually everything you need to publish a Kindle e-book can be found on the Internet for free, if you know where to look. Having this information gathered in one place is what gives this book its value.

Calling this document a book is a stretch of the imagination. It's an article. Something you might find in Writer's Digest or on a Writer's Forum. It isn't about how to write your book, or how to promote it. It's about how to get it published. This is a simple, no "BS" guide on how to publish your book on the Kindle platform, and sell it on Amazon—and to do it for practically nothing.

First off, it's a lot easier to set up an e-book than it is to set up a print version. This is because the layout isn't nearly as complicated. You don't have to worry about page numbering, headers and footers, type fonts, widows and orphans, etc. These things are not a problem with the Kindle because of the way the e-book reader re-flows the text. All you really need to do is to get your text into the right format and then upload it to the Kindle conversion program. If you're disciplined enough to have written a novel, getting it into the Kindle Store shouldn't present much of a problem. Writing the novel was by far the hardest part.

Website:

There are a few things you need to take care of before you upload your first Kindle document. These things are not just related to the Kindle, but to publishing in general. Opening a bank account, getting a business license, (optional) and setting up your own website should be in place before you think about getting listed on Amazon.

If you haven't already done it, get a domain name. This isn't expensive. You can register your domain name for about $10 a year, less if you pay a couple of years in advance. Don't neglect to do this. You hardly ever see a movie or book that doesn't have a website promoting it. Where else can you advertise your novel, 24 hours a day, in full color, with sound and video, for about $60 a year? You can't. And you can't afford not to have your own domain and website.

Do this as soon as possible. Getting the domain name you want may turn out to be harder than you think. Unless your book has a very unusual title, "Breeding Dinosaurs For Fun And Profit" you'll probably find that your first choice for a domain name may already be taken. True, www.BreedingDinosaurs.com is available, (I checked) but mostly because it has such an odd-ball name. As soon as you have a working title, start looking for a domain name. There's a whole batch of new domain extensions available, (.tv, .info, .org, .mobi, .me, .biz) but, ".com" is the one you're going to want. This has always been the most popular and everyone expects to hear, "dot com" at the end of your domain name. All of the major Internet hosting sites have search engines that will allow you to check and see if the name you're trying to get is available.

Don't forget to get your own (real or pen) name registered while you're at it. If you have a common last name, this may not be possible. I have www.RandyBenjamin.com, www.AnomalyTheNovel.com and www.AsherDan.com registered. The AsherDan.com domain is being parked. This means I own it, but it's not being hosted right now. Hosting (I use godaddy.com) costs me about $50 a year, per domain. Parking is usually free.

You can get free hosting at websites such as Tripod.com, but I'd really recommend not doing this. These free hosting sites don't look very professional. When readers log onto these sites, they are presented with banner ads advertising everything from Viagra to new car loans. This says, "Hey, I'm doing this as a hobby." If you really are doing this as a hobby, then the free websites are fine. But if you're serious about your writing, you need to present a professional image to your readers. Having banner ads popping up when someone logs on to your website says exactly the opposite.

My latest fiction novel is called, "The Anomaly." I started looking for an, "Anomaly" domain before I wrote the first page. What I found was that just about everything concerning, 'Anomaly' was already taken. I ended up settling on, www.AnomalyTheNovel.com which is OK, but it definitely wasn't my first choice. I also registered www.AnomalyTheMovie.com while I was at it. I know—but it was only $10, and, "Hey," I can dream can't I?

Once you have the domain name you want, you still have to design a website. I won't even try to get into the basics of web design here other than to say, if you can't do it yourself, have it done. It's not all that hard, especially with the design tools provided by most hosting services. But if you don't feel qualified, farm it out. You should be able to have a website built for a few hundred dollars. This will be money well spent.

You've probably heard that books sold on your own website are the most profitable. There's no doubt about that. Unfortunately, this is not where you'll be making most of your sales. Your website is where you'll be promoting your book. Sure, you'll sell a few books there, but for most of us, our website is where we promote our books, not sell them.

Your website can consist of blogs, pictures, sample chapters, audio sound bites, promotions, front and back book covers, coming events, etc. This is where you'll create a, "buzz" for your book. The majority of sales will come from on-line book sellers and the biggest fish in this pond is Amazon. Amazon sells an average of 1.5 million books a day. You want to make sure that your book is included in these statistics. Besides, the Kindle is an Amazon product. And that's the platform we're interest in.

Kindle DTP: (Digital Text Platform)

The Kindle e-book reader first saw the light of day on November 19th, 2007. The initial supply sold out in six hours. E-books and readers have been around for years but they've never made much of an impact in book sales. Early e-book readers had a lot of problems. They were bulky, there wasn't a lot of content for them, and they had tiny backlit screens that were nearly impossible to read in direct sunlight. Worst of all, they were expensive.

Amazon's Kindle has solved most of these problems. "Expensive" is the one stickler they've yet to overcome, but they're working on it. With production increasing throughout the first half of 2008, the base price of the Kindle dropped from $399 to $359. Hopefully, this trend will continue. When it can be purchased for under $100, look out. Increase the number of Kindle owners, and you'll increase the number of books sold proportionately.

With the success of the Kindle, Amazon has been clamoring for new content. Finally, here is a market that self-publishing authors can participate in.

Before you can sell your book on Amazon, you'll need to sign up with Kindle's publishing program. You can do this easily over the Internet by logging onto Kindle's signup page located at: http:// www.opaauthorservices.com/kindle_signup.htm. You'll be asked for the usual…name, address and phone number. Because you'll be receiving royalties, you'll also need to provide your social security number and bank account information. (For direct royalty deposits.) It's about like signing up for a credit card. It's no big deal, it just takes a little time. If you already have a publishing company, you may want to use it instead of your personal information.

One thing to remember about the Kindle program is that you're only giving Amazon the rights to distribute the Kindle version of your novel. You're not getting married to them. You can release your book in any other format you choose and sell it through other on-line retailers and store fronts—even other e-book retailers. Amazon may be the biggest fish in the pond, but they're certainly not the only one.

Early on, Amazon setup a website http:// dtp.amazon.com/mn/signin for authors to upload their novels and integrate them into the Kindle Store. To do this, Amazon uses what they call DTP (digital text platform) to convert the author's text into the Kindle format. Early versions of the DTP software had a lot of, "bugs." By mid-year, 2008, most of these problems had been discovered and fixed. Still, getting your novel uploaded and converted can be a little…awkward. I'm using, "novel" here, but you can publish anything from a company brochure, to your grocery list.

To start with, the Kindle conversion software doesn't like PDF (Portable Document File) files. As you may already know, PDF files are the industry standard when getting a book setup for traditional printing. This book was originally published in the Kindle format only. I had to make a lot of changes to release it in a paperback version. With the current version of the DTP, you'll have to forget PDFs altogether. The DTP software can convert other file types though. The file type that seems to work best with Kindle's current conversion software is HTML. Since most of us use Microsoft Word, I'm going to show you how to convert Words, "doc" output to HTML. It's easy.

Before you do it though, you'll need to modify your page layout. Because the Kindle re-flows text, page numbering isn't needed and will screw things up. Bring up your novel in Word. At the top of the page, click on <view> and then <headers and footers>. Delete any page numbers and headers and footers you previously installed. The Kindle will renumber your pages on-the-fly depending on the size of font the reader selected.

This brings up two serious problems for nonfiction writers. The problems are indexing and Table of Contents. It's the re-flowing of text and varying page positions that make these problems so hard to deal with. If you write fiction, this shouldn't be a problem. But if you're writing non-fiction and need to reference individual pages, you're going to be up-a-creek until the DTP team adds this option to the conversion software. In some cases you can get around this by "linking" to text later on in your document. But this gets complicated the more links you include.

If you have a chapter index, one thing you might consider doing is to put links to the various chapters in your book, when readers click on these links, it will take them directly to that chapter's beginning. This would allow them to go to any chapter no matter where it's located. This will work for 'tables" and "charts" too. You might also put a link at the end of each chapter to take you back to the chapter, "index." This is one way to navigate to different sections of your document, but it's really just a "patch" to get you by until the DTP designers come up with something better. I hope that something is a good PDF conversion program! Once you've removed your page numbers, you're ready to save your file and start the conversion to the Kindle format. HTML stands for, "Hyper Text Markup Language." This is the programming language your Internet browser (Internet Explorer, Netscape, Fire Fox, etc.) uses. One other thing I should mention here is that even though I'm using HTML as the file extension, the, "L" is usually not included in the file extension tag. This is because early versions of Windows only provided three digits for the file extension. So if you view the, "details" of a file and only see HTM at the end of it, don't worry...you're fine. I'll continue to use the full HTML tag here, but HTM will work just as well. You may see lower case, "html" too. Both are fine.

The easiest way to create this file in Word is to save your text as an HTML file type instead of Word's standard, "doc" file. Here's how to do this. Bring up your novel and click on <file> and <save as> (not save) at the top left of the page. A new menu will appear. At the bottom of this menu, you'll find two blank boxes. Move the curser to the lower box, (save as file type) and click on the down arrow on the right side of the box. This will bring up a list of file types you can use when saving your document.

There are two file types associated with HTML. Click on the one that says, "Web Page, filtered." Word adds a lot of extra formatting commands into its files that don't need to be included in the HTML file we'll be converting. The, "filtering" option removes most of these unneeded commands. IE: It cleans up the extra garbage that, "Word" includes in the file conversion. The blank box above the file type is where you enter your file name.

The top part of this menu displays the various directories on your hard drive. I created a separate directory for my Kindle files and use it for everything that has to do with my Kindle project. This includes the manuscript without page numbers in both the .doc and .HTML versions. This way, I won't have to worry about overwriting any other files by accident.

When you save your HTML filtered file, you should give it a new file name. In my case, my original Word file was called, "The Anomaly." I changed this to, "K_The Anomaly" for the Kindle version. The K at the beginning lets me know that this is the Kindle file. The one without page numbers, headers and footers. The, "HTML" file extension is automatically added to the end of the file when you use the <save as>, "web page filtered" menu choice.

The HTML file you just saved is the inside of your book, the text. You'll also need to upload the book's cover. This is a different file altogether. You may have written your book in Word, but you most likely designed the cover using a graphics program. The actual designing of the cover is something I'll just touch on here since there are so many ways to go about it. Here's how I designed mine.

I had a basic idea of what I wanted the cover to look like when I started. I wanted it to be very sparse and not cluttered. The book's cover is your poster. It has to grab the reader's attention right off. When I'm at a book store, the cover is the first thing I notice about a book. If it gets my attention, I'll pick it up and read the description on the back. This is about all you have to work with in selling your book…the cover and the description. On-line, the cover is even more important. It must generate enough interest that the potential buyer will take the time to read the description associated with it. You only have 4,000 characters for your book's description. Not words—characters. This may sound like a lot, but it won't take you long to realize, it's not.

My, "Anomaly" cover consists of a catchy graphic, (an atom) the title, my pen name, and a short phrase, "SOME DOORS SHOULD BE BOLTED SHUT—FOREVER!" The title, "The Anomaly" is set in jagged blood red type which gives the book the feel that it's a scary read. The phrase and author's name are in white. All of this sits against a jet black background which really makes it stand out. I'm not a cover designer by any means, but with a little effort, I was able to produce a pretty catchy cover. You can view it here, http://www.AnomalyTheNovel.com.

To design the cover I used an inexpensive graphics program called, "Paint Shop Pro." I'll use it in the following examples, but graphics programs are very similar so whatever program you're using will most likely work in much the same way. Unlike PhotoShop, Paint Shop Pro doesn't have a difficult learning curve associated with it. And, it produces files that can be directly uploaded to Kindle's DTP.

You can save your cover design as either a TIF or JPG file for inclusion into Amazon's data base. The TIF file is a non-compressed file and has higher resolution. This is important if you're going to print it, but for displaying on a computer monitor, JPG is just fine.

A back cover isn't necessary for the Kindle Store display. This is another advantage of publishing in the Kindle format. There's less work involved in almost every aspect of the production and design process.

An important thing to think about when designing your cover is that the image of your book on Amazon is small. If you have a lot of text on the cover, people will have a hard time reading it. Color and graphics are the best way to draw attention to your book. Whether on-line or in a book store, you're competing with thousands of other authors so having a knocked out cover design is critical. Your cover has to catch the reader's eye or you're sunk before you even get started.

Image size is important as well. Most graphics software will allow you to work in different image resolutions. This is simply the number of pixels displayed per inch. In the print world, this is referred to as 'dpi' or dots per inch. Laser printers are usually rated at 300, 600, or 1,200 dots per inch. Monitors display about 72 pixels per inch. Amazon wants the cover image you'll be using on your display page to be between 500 and 1,200 pixels on the longest side.

Of course, you want a catchy cover on Amazon's display page, but you'll also want this cover included at the beginning of your Kindle e-book. This cover needs to be in black and white, not the color version that appears at the Kindle Store. This is because the Kindle only displays in black and white. Actually, it uses a low resolution gray scale for graphics. The Kindle is excellent at displaying text, but its graphics are limited.

Using Paint Shop Pro, it's easy to convert your color cover to grayscale. Start by loading your cover into Paint Shop Pro. You'll see a menu choice at the top of the page called, "image." Click on it and a submenu will appear. One of the choices displayed will be, "grayscale." All you have to do is click on this option and your cover will be converted to grayscale. It's that simple.

One more step is needed before you save this inside-the-book cover. While the cover on Amazon's display page needed to be between 500 and 1,200 pixels on the longest side, the cover for your e-book has to be much smaller. This is because the display area on the Kindle is much smaller than your computer's monitor. Amazon recommends a size of between 400 and 600 pixels for the longest side.

Sizing your cover is easy with Paint Shop Pro. In the menu at the top of the page look for <image> and then <resize>. This choice will allow you to expand or reduce your cover image. You'll also find a button in this section that will tell you what the current image size is. It may take a little experimenting, but it's not hard. I spent about five minutes resizing my cover. Once sized, you can save it by clicking on <file> and then <save as>. Be sure to give the image a new name so you can import it into your manuscript. I used, "K_cover_gray.jpg" as a file name. The name you chose should differentiate between your color (display) and grayscale (e-book) covers.

Attaching the grayscale image to your manuscript is something you'll only need to do in the Kindle version of your novel. This is another reason I like to keep all of my Kindle files in their own directory. Load the HTML version of your novel into Word and make sure you're at the beginning of your document. Now, click on <insert> at the top of the page. A menu will appear. Click on <picture> and then <from file>. A directory of your hard drive will appear. If you don't see your grayscale cover file, move through the directories until you do. Once you find it, click on it. You should now see it at the beginning of your document. Of course, it looks great on your computer, but it won't look that good when displayed on the Kindle.

Your computer has 256 shades of gray, the Kindle has 4. Now, save your document (HTML file type) and your cover will be included in your Kindle e-book.

Here's a tip. If you have a Kindle to experiment with, you can copy the grayscale cover to the Kindle over your USB port and see what it looks like. If it's too dark or too light, use your graphics program to enhance it until it looks the best on your Kindle. Save this copy and use it for your e-book's cover. This way, you'll be assured of having the best image possible.

At this point, you should have three files saved in your Kindle directory. The text file, the color cover file, and the grayscale cover file. If so, you're ready to start uploading your book for conversion. Log onto the Kindle DTP. You'll be asked for your ID and password.

Here's one of the best things about the Kindle publishing platform. Not only can you publish your book for free, you don't even have to purchase any proofs. You can proof it using the preview section of the DTP platform. Once it's exactly the way you want it, just press, "Publish" and the final version will be uploaded to Amazon and placed in the Kindle Store. It usually takes from 24 to 72 hours before it goes on line.

If you decide later that you want to change something, you just upload the changes and your updates will take the place of the original files. This is a very important feature that many Kindle owners and even some authors aren't aware of.

As an example, it's been about eight weeks since I first published this book on Amazon. Because of the limited number of Kindle owners, I decided to publish a paperback version as well. This consisted mostly of updating the original e-book and converting it into PDF format for printing. All of the updates I'm making for the print version will also be uploaded to the Kindle version. The neat thing about owning a Kindle is that anyone who has already purchased the original e-book will be able to download the updated version for free. All a reader has to do is to download it. As long as it's the same title, Amazon allows you to download any updates for free. If you've purchased a "how-to" book, be sure to check occasionally to see if any updates are available.

As an author, this allows you to keep your books current. It's also important in the print world though the reader has to purchase additional print copies to get the updates. Free updates are a great selling point for e-books. As an author, you can update your print version at any time so that new purchasers of your book will always have the most recent copy. I'll be using Amazon's CreateSpace to print and distribute my paperback copies. They take care of everything.

All I have to purchase is a proof copy. About $2.85 and shipping for this book.

Back to the book design…something you may not have considered is that all of the graphics and fonts you use in your cover design need to be royalty free. This means, be sure that they are not copyrighted. Don't just copy a picture you saw on the Internet and use it in your book unless you contact the owner of that picture and get permission to use it. Ask for a release, and get it in writing. If you use a quote, get a release from the person you quoted as well. If they are no longer with us, (as in…dead) check to see if their estate or publisher will allow you to quote them. Speaking of copyrights…you can register your manuscript with the electronic copyright office in Washington DC by logging onto http:// www.copyright.gov/register/. The cost is $35 per electronic filing. Instructions for filing are on the website.

Working with the DTP:

If you've finished designing your cover, saved your manuscript as an HTML file including the grayscale cover, it's time to get your book online. Bring up the Internet and log onto the Kindle DTP program. Here, you'll find a menu with five choices across the top. These are, My Shelf, My Reports, My Account, Help, and Sign Out. "My Shelf" is where you'll enter information about your book. We'll start here. There are three steps involved in publishing your book. These are, (1) Enter Product Details, (2) Upload & Preview, and (3) Enter Price. When these are completed, press the, "Publish" button, and you're finished.

The first thing you're asked in step one is to enter the ISBN number. Having an ISBN number is not all that important for Kindle only sales. I have an ISBN number on the print version of, "How To Publish Anything On Amazon's Kindle" but I didn't include one on the e-book version. Amazon will assign a special identifier for your book to track sales and determine royalties. If you have one though and want to use it, now is the time to enter it. Otherwise, leave it blank.

Next, you're asked for the books title. Enter your title here.

The description of your book is the next step. This is probably the most important part of the entire publishing process. You're limited to 4,000 characters. Not much when you consider you're describing the whole book. I'd advise you to write several descriptions using Word first, then combine the best parts of them into one description and rework it until it conforms to the 4,000 character limit. Word's <tools> <word count> menu choice will give you the character count as well as the word count.

Remember, you're up against every top selling author in the world, so make it good. The cover may have gotten a buyer's attention, but it's the description that closes the deal.

Once you have the description like you want it, **print it**. DON'T copy/paste it to the DTP. Now, use this printout as a model and re-type it word-for-word into the description box in the DTP. To double check that you didn't make any mistakes, highlight what you just typed, and copy/paste it to a blank Word document. This way you can easily check for spelling errors. If you find any misspelled words, correct them in the DTP description. DON'T copy/paste the corrections from the Word doc back to the DTP. This may cause problems.

I know, this seems like a stupid way to enter your description into the DTP box…but there's a reason to do it this way. Why not just copy/paste the description from Word to the DTP to begin with? The problem is…Window's copy/paste function inserts weird characters into your text that only show up once your description goes online at Amazon. You won't see these weird characters until it's too late.

I learned this the hard way. I wrote my first description of, "The Anomaly" in Word and pasted it into the DTP. When it went online at Amazon, all of the, "quotes" displayed as diamonds <>. They looked fine in the description box, but they didn't convert correctly when Amazon published them on my book's display page. It took me quite a while to figure out exactly what had happened. The last thing I suspected was that it was a problem with the Window's copy/paste function. Just be sure you actually type your description into the description box on the DTP. Use Word to spell-check it, but don't copy/paste any corrections. Type them in.

The next thing you'll be asked for is the Publisher. If you have one, type the name in here, if not, leave it blank. Two more boxes complete the left section of the display. Language, most of us will select English here, and Publishing Date. If your book has a publishing date, enter it here, if not, just enter today's date.

On the right hand side of the display, you'll find several more questions. The first is, Categories. When you click on add/edit, a list of categories will come up. Click on any that your book fits into. You can add more if you need to.

The next box is, Authors. Click on add/edit and enter your name, or pen name here. Now we're ready for search words. These are words that people can search on to find your book in Amazon's database. Use words that describe your book. The Anomaly is a sci-fi thriller, so I used, sci-fi, science fiction, horror, thriller, King, Koontz, mystery, and scary, Use anything you think a reader might enter in order to find a book like yours.

The next box is, Edition Number. If this is a series, enter the number that this particular book is in that series. If it's the first book, enter a 1. If it's not part of a series, just leave it blank. If it is part of a series, the next box is where you enter the series title. Below that, you can put in the Series Volume. If none of these apply, leave all of them blank.

The last thing to do in this section is to upload your color cover image. This is the image that potential buyers will see when they find your title. There's an icon of a camera in the center of the page with, "Product Image" written above it. Below it is a button with, "Upload Image" on it. Click on this button.

A menu will come up that says, "Product Image Upload." You'll also see a blank box with a, "Browse" button to the right of it. Click on it and the directory of your hard drive will appear. Navigate to the place where your book's cover image is stored. You should already have sized it earlier, (500 to 1,200 pixels) so all you have to do is click on it, and it will be uploaded to the DTP and placed on your book's display page in the Kindle Store.

Tip: Most of the authors on the Kindle forums state that the size isn't all that important. If in doubt, keep it the actual size of the book's cover. The Kindle DTP will automatically resize it to fit. I went ahead and resized mine to Amazon's specifications so I can't be sure of this. But if what you use doesn't look good online, all it will cost you is a little time to do the resizing.

That takes care of section (1) "Enter Product Details." If you decide to change something later, just make the changes and upload the new files. No charges are incurred and the changes will show up in less than 72 hours. My changes showed up in less than ten hours.

Now, it's time to get your text uploaded, converted, and previewed. Click on the (2) Upload & Preview button. This is the second step in the publishing process. A new menu will appear that says, "Upload & Preview Book."

Below this is a box labeled, Media Location. To its right is a, "browse" button. If you click on the, "browse" button, a directory of your hard drive will appear. Here, you can select the file(s) you need to convert into the Kindle format. These files should be in the, "Kindle" directory you created earlier.

This is also where the DTP starts to show its limitations. One problem I had right off the bat was in getting my text image, the grayscale one, to appear at the top of my e-book.

When dealing with HTML files, you need all of the graphics to reside in the same directory as your HTML text file. If you are including a grayscale cover of your book at the beginning of your text, Amazon wants it uploaded as a separate file. This means you now have two files to upload to complete your text…the grayscale cover (jpg) and the text (HTML). But…Amazon only wants to deal with a single file. In order to do this, you'll need to, "zip" the two files into one file. If you have other image files in your manuscript, include them in this, "zip" file too.

First, make sure that the files you're working with are all in the same directory on your hard drive. Zipping files may be something that you're not familiar with. Zipping simply means to combine two or more files into one, "compressed" file. Zipping does several things. First, because it compresses files, it saves hard drive space. It does this by using special algorithms that are able to delete duplicated characters in a file. It restores the deleted characters when the file is unzipped. Compressed, "zipped" files also transmit much faster over the Internet. Text files can often be compressed by a factor of ten or more. This means that a 100,000 byte file reduced by a factor of ten would only be 10,000 bytes in length.

Not only does this save space, it saves time. If it took 10 minutes to transmit an uncompressed file, with 10 to 1 compression, it would only take one minute to transmit the same file. Amazon deals with millions of files a day. By compressing, or zipping files, enormous amounts of time and space are saved. It's also easier for them to work with one file as apposed to many.

There are several, "zipping" programs available for free on the Net. Bring up Google and search for, "Free zipping software." One of the most popular commercial zipping programs is WinZip. You can find it here, http:// www.winzip.com/index.htm. There are instructions on their website on how to use it. The last time I checked, the basic version was priced at $29.95. There's a free trial version available as well.

WinZip is a commercial program but you'll find several free zipping programs in the Google search too. They all work in much the same way. A few utility programs include zipping functions as well. System Suite and System Mechanics are two I'd highly recommend.

Once you've zipped your text file (HTML) and the grayscale cover (jpg) image into a single file, you're ready to upload it to the DTP. In the (2) "Upload and Preview File" section, click on your zipped file and it will upload to Kindle's DTP for conversion and preview. This took less than a minute for my file on a high-speed DSL connection. The conversion took about 30 seconds.

Once your file has been converted, you can preview it on your computer immediately. There's a, "preview" button just to the right of the, "upload" button on the

DTP. The preview software is pretty good, but not perfect. There's really no substitute for viewing your book on an actual Kindle. Graphics are the source of most problems. Because the Kindle has such a low number of gray shades, they won't look anything like they do on your computer. If you can tweak them on your Kindle before uploading them, you'll be sure to have the best image possible.

One of the nicest things about the DTP is that you can make changes, and then view the changes in a matter of minutes. There's no charge for this, just the time it takes to upload your changes. I tried out several things before I finally got it the way I wanted. Once you have it right, you're ready for step three.

The third step in the publishing process is to set a price for your book. Click on the third icon in the publishing menu, "Enter Price." This will bring up a new screen with only one box in it. Before you enter your price, make sure that you've ran the numbers and have nailed down the best price for your book.

There are no printing charges associated with e-books. No shipping to worry about either. These are two of the reasons that e-books are usually priced much lower than their printed cousins. The print version of, "The Anomaly" retails for $13.83. I decided to charge $5.99 for the e-book. Amazon discounted it to $4.79. Amazon pays e-book authors 35% of the retail price of their books. The author sets the price. Even if Amazon discounts the book, the author is still paid on the retail selling price. The price you're about to enter now.

Hopefully, Amazon will discount your book as much as possible. I'd be happy if they sold mine for a penny.

The lower the price, the more likely someone will be to buy it. You make the same royalty, no matter how much they discount it. I've seen a lot of e-books listed for under a dollar. This seems a little drastic to me, but maybe it's working for that author. You're not stuck with whatever price you decide on. You can change it at any time. That's one of the nice things about e-book publishing for the Kindle. You can make changes at any time and have them implemented in less than 72 hours. For free.

As short as this e-book is, I decided that I would price it accordingly. I chose $2.49. At this rate, I make 87 cents per copy. That seemed like a fair price to charge for a book of this length. Amazon discounted it to $1.99. I like that fact that it's less than $2. It just sounds better.

The paperback version is priced at $6.25. This gives me a profit of $1.50 per book. Amazon will set a minimum price that you can't go below. On this book it was $6.10. I originally planned to charge $5.25. You won't know the minimum until the last step in the publishing process. I doubt that many authors will have a problem in pricing their books too low. More likely, it will be just the opposite.

If you've followed me so far, you should be ready for the final step in the publishing process. In the first step, you uploaded your color cover for the Amazon display page and filled in the product details. In the second step, you uploaded your text file and grayscale cover image. In the third step, you decided what the selling price for your e-book should be and entered it into the, "Enter Price" box.

At this point, you need to stop and consider everything you've done so far. If you're satisfied that everything has been done to the best of your ability, then you're ready to publish your book. Click on the, "Publish" button. This sets into motion all of the things necessary for Amazon to include your book in their database and display it in the Kindle Store.

Amazon says it will take up to 72 hours before your book will show up in the Kindle Store and for sale. This can vary. My book was online in about 12 hours. I'm guessing though that even though I could view it, it wasn't yet integrated into the various databases and search engines. It was actually, "for sale" about 36 hours later. I made a few changes after my book was online (the description problem I mentioned earlier) and these changes showed up the next day.

Once you start to get sales, you can track them using, "My Reports." This is another function of the DTP software. Amazon changed the reports section sometime in June. It was much more helpful before the change. You used to be able to enter a date range to see how many books you sold during that range. That was really nice in that, if you ran a promotion, you could see how much of a difference it made using the specified date range.

Unfortunately, the new reports section has changed this so you can only see sales listed over the full month. They dropped the daily sales breakdown. These monthly reports can be downloaded in Microsoft's "Excel" format. They list sales by title, number sold, selling price, and total royalty paid. It's OK, but not nearly as nice as it used to be. Amazon pays royalties in two month intervals. This is kind of confusing at first.

Here are two examples. Royalties accrued in the month of January are paid on March 1st. If your book came out on June 10th then you'll receive royalties for all June sales on August 1st. Basically, the billing cycle is two months behind. Amazon also requires you to have accumulated at least $10 in royalties before they'll credit your bank account. Once this limit is reached, you'll be paid on the next billing cycle. The electronic transfer is free. You can request a check, but you'll be charged for it.

When you log onto the Kindle DTP, you'll find a, "help" section called the Digital Text Platform Support Center. It consists of several user forums plus a knowledge base. On the forums, you can post questions to either the Kindle administrators or to other Kindle authors. The forum is very interesting. The posts go back to the very beginning when things weren't nearly as good as they are now. It's easy to see how the DTP has improved with time.

The forums work well, but it means that you won't be getting instant answers to your questions. It usually takes a day or two.

There is NO live support. Of course, that's one of the reasons why you can publish your book for practically nothing. It's up to you to track down the answer to why something isn't working. There's NO hand holding and NO Rep to answer your questions. But there's NO drain on your pocketbook either.

This short book (there I go, calling it a book again) is an example of how quickly something can be written, published, and, 'For Sale' in the Kindle Store. I started writing this on a Sunday afternoon, six days before I was to give a publishing workshop for our local writer's guild. I finished it on Thursday afternoon. I spent about an hour designing the cover. I didn't have time to do anything fancy, I figured I could improve on it later and upload the, "improved" version when I had more time. I only needed the front cover at the time because the back cover isn't displayed on Amazon and being an e-book, no back cover was necessary.

I uploaded the manuscript to the DTP Thursday night and it appeared at the Kindle Store Friday afternoon. That was cutting it close. (The workshop was the following day.) I had gone from a blank screen to a finished e-book in less than a week...published, online, and for sale.

You are reading an updated version right now. Updating is an ongoing process as things change with the DTP software. The exciting thing is...e-books have arrived. Over the next few years, there's going to be an explosion in electronic publishing. Publishing is going to go through a change much like we saw in the music business. Major labels no longer have complete control over the artist's choice of music and its production. Independent record companies have sprung up everywhere, many started by the artists themselves. The same thing has happened in the movie industry with small production companies producing many of today's movies.

Computers and the Internet have made much of this possible. Computers have brought the costs of making records, movies, and now, publishing books within the reach of creative people everywhere. Amazon's Kindle has given new authors an opportunity that was unheard of just a few years ago. The doors are open—it's up to us to walk through them.

Update added on 11/13/2008
An experiment using the Kindle Platform to gather reviews

I've written several non-fiction books all self published and distributed through the 23 newspapers that carried my "Internet Guide" column. But I'd never attempted a fiction novel. It took me a little over a year to finish the manuscript. It totaled 330 pages. I subscribe to several Yahoo publishing forums. (POD Publishers is my favorite.) All of the authors and publishers on this forum preach that every book needs to be professionally edited. I agree 100%.

The problem is…for a self published author, this can be a very expensive undertaking. Anywhere from $3 to $5 a page and up, mostly UP. I wanted my manuscript to be as good as I could make it before I had it professionally edited. I also wanted to know what worked in the novel and what didn't. I didn't want to spend money having pages edited that were going to thrown out later. So I developed a plan to get reviews by releasing the pre-edited novel as a Kindle e-book.

I figured that the sales would be small enough (unknown writer, no advertising) that it wouldn't matter in the short run if the book wasn't up to snuff and I'd get reviews from real "readers" not just friends and family. Then I realized that I would be selling something that I knew could be better and that would be "cheating" my readers. So, I decided to give away the e-book in return for reviews.

The first thing I found was that Amazon doesn't allow you to give away e-books easily. They won't just let you buy the book and send it to anyone, at least, not in the Kindle version. You have to have a Kindle registered at Amazon before you can even purchase a Kindle e-book. And, you can only buy one book of a given title per Kindle. I did get a break though in that; Amazon discounted my $5.99 book to $4.79. What I ended up doing was running a contest saying that I'd give away one book a day until the end of the year. This started back in August. Since I couldn't give the actual e-books away I gave away $5 gift certificates, 157 of them! Of course, an Amazon gift certificate is good for anything on Amazon. So if the receiver of the certificate decided to use it towards the purchase of another book, then I was just out the $5.

I only mentioned this contest once on one of the Kindle forums...but the requests came rolling in. After two months I decided that it was pretty stupid to wait until the end of the year to give away all of the e-books, so I ended up taking the first 157 responders and sending them each a $5 gift certificate. On the certificate I asked them to "Please send a review to my website at: http://www.AnomalyTheNovel.com" And told them I wanted to know what they liked and didn't like about the novel. Unfortunately, several people posted their reviews on my Amazon book page instead of sending an email to my website. And I was asking what they didn't like about the book. If I ever do this again, I'll certainly do it differently.

But I did find out what I needed to work on. In fact, I've edited it down to 302 pages. It's much tighter now and an easier read. I'm just about ready for the professional edit. The $785 I spent on gift certificates was well worth it. Actually, because I get back 35% of the $785 (royalties) the final cost of the give-a-way was about $547.

I ended up with 72 reviews. My account showed that 142 books were purchased during the two months it took me to give out the certificates. So that wasn't too bad either. If only 15 people used the gift certificate for something else, I can't complain about that percentage.

This experiment would have been far too expensive to try with paperback books. The paperback version of The Anomaly sells for $13.83. To give out 157 paperback books would have cost me $2,355.00. ($15 gift certificates) I'd have gotten back $3.49 each in royalties, for an over all expenditure of $1,807.00, compared to $547 for the e-book.

Speaking of reviews...since you've purchased this "publishing" book, I assume you are considering publishing a Kindle e-book of your own. Don't underestimate just how important reviews can be. Take them seriously. I only have two reviews on this book so far, (I've sold about 40 copies in two months.) one good, and one bad. I'm sure the bad review has cost me sales. With a profit of only 87 cents a book, every sale is important.

My gripe is that the bad review wasn't a fair review. The reader was looking for a book that would solve a problem that there really isn't any solution too. He wants to transfer a Microsoft Power Point presentation to the Kindle format. This can't be done. So, no, this book didn't help him with his problem. But why trash a book because it doesn't do the impossible? His gripe should have been with the people who wrote the DPT software, not me. What he should do is to complain to them. Though I don't think that what he wants to do will ever be possible.

It hurts to get a bad review. And when it's an undeserved one, it hurts all the more. Here's another example.

I have a terrible review of, "The Anomaly" on its Amazon review page. The review starts by saying, "First off, I haven't read this book." What an idiot! Sorry, but he's just stupid. Then he goes on to compare the book (that he hasn't read) to a computer game. Half-Life I believe. I've never ever seen Half-life. But he trashes the book saying it's a rip-off of the game. For the topper, he says that $23 for this book is another rip-off. The e-book costs $4.79 and the paperback version is $13.83. Where did he get the $23? I did a search on Amazon and sure enough, there is another book with the same title and it's listed for $23.

So this guy is trashing a book that he hasn't even read and it turns out that it's not even my book! Yet, I get the bad review. I hope people like this aren't able to reproduce.

It's too bad that most people only post reviews when they "don't" like something. On a $2 e-book like this one, there's not much incentive either way. But when you, as an author, spend hundreds of hours and thousands of dollars trying to get your novel off the ground, reviews can really make a difference.

If this book helps you out, post a review. If not...forget you ever read it. Just kidding! Seriously, just remember that what you say does make a difference. Good or bad, just be fair when you write it. You won't fully appreciate this until your own book is on Amazon.

I'm sorry if I appear to be promoting my own books in these examples. But that's because I know exactly what's happening with them. It's not second hand information. When I try something new, I know if it worked or not, and to what extent.

Hopefully, I can save you a few dollars and some time along the way.

I said in the beginning that this book wasn't about promotion...but logically, that's the next stage in the publishing process. As I explore it, I'll let you know what I find out. I'm always looking new ways to get a book into the main stream without spending a lot of money. This doesn't mean another book is in the making, just "free" add-ons to this one.

If you have anything you'd like me to include in the next update, let me know at:

http://randy@randybenjamin.com
http://www.asher@AnomalyTheNovel.com.

You can download updated versions of "How To Publish Anything On Amazon's Kindle" at the Kindle store for free, anytime. The paperback will have the same updates, but unfortunately, Amazon doesn't give them away. That's another advantage the Kindle has over its paperback counterpart.

I'll put the date of each update in the book's description section at the Kindle Store. If you see a new date, log into your Amazon account and redownload it from your computer. Be sure to delete the version stored in your Kindle first. Then the new download will replace it. You can do this from the "Content" manager.

Thank you for your purchase. I hope you've found the information I've provided worthwhile.

Randy Benjamin

* Author's Notes *

Randy Benjamin has been a computer consultant for 35 years. His first venture into writing was in 1995 when he sold several articles to Music Row magazine in Nashville TN. The series detailed how computers and digital technology were changing the way that music was being created. Over the next several years, writing began to play a much larger roll in his life.

In 1998 he started a newspaper column called, "The Internet Guide" which was syndicated by 23 newspapers in three Midwestern states. This column spawned two books, "The Internet Guide Handbook" and "More of the Internet Guide." The Internet Guide ran until 2007 when he decided that he'd rather work on novels full time.

In March of 2007, he closed his consulting business and wrote the last of 491 Internet Guide articles. Now approaching 62 years of age, he writes full time working on novels and writing articles for magazines world wide.

His hobbies are fishing and designing solar projects for his home. Presently, his computers and lighting system are solar powered. His goal is to get off the power grid entirely.

He lives on a small lake in southern Indiana with a dog named Mufeoso.